SECTION

ONE

Guidelines

CONTENTS - SECTION ONE

INTRODUCTION

SOME THINGS TO CONSIDER: -

○   It is unlikely that effective learning will take place in an undisciplined environment.

○   Pupils and parents appreciate a classroom which is well managed and which gives a feeling of security.

○   In a culture where problems appear to be on the increase, teachers need techniques and guidelines to help them maintain proper working conditions.

○   We recognise that many pupils who behave inappropriately at school are experiencing problems at home and that these are beyond our control. We should not, however, let that stop us helping pupils to learn new, more acceptable ways of behaving at school.

○   Pupils with challenging behaviour are generally not "troublesome" on a one-to-one basis, away from their peer audience.

○   Pupils who display problem behaviour are best dealt with from a shared perspective. These problems need a "team approach".

○   We must recognise that a child's behaviour is generally not the teacher's fault and support, if needed, should be offered on a colleague support basis.

○ Some pupils may have a collection of inappropriate behaviours. It is important, however, to work on only a few at a time and not overwhelm the child.

○ Behavioural change takes time and success should be defined as a decrease over time in frequency and intensity of targeted behaviours.

* In this book, pupils are referred to as "he" regardless of gender.

USEFUL TIPS

These will be things you do already, but this list may serve as a useful reminder, especially to new staff.

- ○ Respect every student.

- ○ Be reliable and consistent. If you say you will do something, then do it.

- ○ Do not leave the classroom unattended. Try always to be there before the pupils arrive.

- ○ Never take pupils out of school without enough competent help.

- ○ Only ever ignore unacceptable behaviour as part of a planned approach.

- ○ Never favour one student over another. Your reaction to a behaviour should be the same for each pupil.

- ○ Seek support from colleagues.

- ○ Develop a strong, calm, voice.

- ○ Show zero tolerance for "put downs".

- ○ Keep pupils with potential behavioural problems busy at all times.

○   Do not try to speak over pupils. Ensure that they are quiet before you begin.

○   Expect to be "tested" by pupils. They will invariably see "how far they can go".

○   The best classroom is one where teachers have detailed working knowledge of each pupil.

○   The more enthusiastic you are, the more enthusiastic the pupils will be and this will lead to better classroom management.

○   Never assume that children are clear about what is expected of them. We sometimes need to specifically teach skills which we take for granted. We need, therefore, to develop approaches which will teach pupils: -

   •   How to attract attention appropriately, without persistent calling out.

   •   How to wait for a turn instead of butting in.

   •   How to sit on the carpet during group time without disrupting others or rolling around.

   •   How to stay in their seats for more than a few minutes.

   •   How to speak quietly, not using inappropriately loud voices.

- How to settle to a task and stay "on task" for a set period of time.

- How to move around the room without disturbing or annoying others.

- How to consider others, using basic social courtesies and cooperative behaviours.

- How to line up outside the classroom without pushing or annoying others.

- How to use respectful language, e.g. "Please", "Thanks", "Can I borrow?", "Excuse me...."

- What to do when they are frustrated, angry or are failing.

GENERAL TIPS FOR CARPET TIME

Think about the seating arrangements:

○   It may be tempting to group potentially disruptive children together but this is rarely productive.

○   Sit potentially disruptive children near to staff and/or with appropriate peers, at the front if possible.

○   Separate class groups, e.g. tables, ability groups, friends.

○   Ensure everyone can see and hear, taking into consideration those with special needs, e.g. poor eyesight, hearing.

○   Consider having a seating plan. It may take some time to find one that is successful.

○   Consider having mats with children's names on. Pupils could make these. Arrange them prior to carpet time, in an arrangement which suits the activity.

Think about the activity:

○   Make carpet activities interactive and fun. Ask lots of questions, use different voices in stories, use props, create opportunities for children to DO things etc.

○ Carpets can be cold, hard and itchy. If this presents itself as an issue, consider providing chairs, cushions or blankets for the children to sit on.

○ Take into account that some pupils may not be comfortable answering questions in a large group situation. Try to overcome this sensitively.

Think about what you are trying to achieve:

○ It is easy to get caught up in trying to achieve perfect behaviour from all pupils, particularly during potentially disruptive times such as carpet time. Try to remember that much of the behaviour which is displayed is out of your control. Your goal should be to get most of the class to behave appropriately most of the time.

○ When feeling stressed, stop and think. Try to stay calm and regain the children's attention before continuing teaching. Continuing with an activity when very few are listening is frustrating for both staff and children.

○ It is the behaviour you are trying to change or manage, not the child. Try to separate the child from the behaviour. This includes positive behaviour as well as negative.

○ If things go wrong, try a joke, a distraction, or total change in activity to break the cycle.

○ When feeling stressed, stop and think. Try to stay calm and regain the children's attention before continuing teaching. Continuing with an activity when very few are listening is frustrating for both staff and children.

○ It is the behaviour you are trying to change or manage, not the child. Try to separate the child from the behaviour. This includes positive behaviour as well as negative.

○ If things go wrong, try a joke, a distraction, or total change in activity to break the cycle.

There are many strategies which can be successful in dealing with undesirable behaviours. Here are a few.

PRIVATELY UNDERSTOOD CUES

After a particular behaviour has been targeted and a more acceptable alternative (e.g. sitting quietly on the carpet) has been outlined and practised, some privately understood cues or signals can be very useful as a reminder.

These might include: -

○ Four fingers extended down like four chair legs on the floor to remind pupils to sit appropriately.

○ Finger to the lips and the fore finger and thumb closing together to convey that the noise needs to be reduced.

○ Crossing two index fingers to remind pupils to cross their legs when sitting on the carpet or in Assembly.

○ Bringing hands together to remind pupils to put their hands still, in laps.

○ Putting index finger to own eyes and pointing back to the front of the room, to remind pupils to "face the front".

○ Give pupils the "Okay" sign, with thumb and forefinger to support and encourage when the pupils remembers the appropriate behaviour.

○ Show positive reinforcement by giving pupils the "thumbs up" sign and / or a wink.

AVOIDING CONFRONTATION IN THE PLAYGROUND

This technique for dealing with inappropriate behaviours depends on clear rules being in place. These rules must be taught, understood and frequent reminders of the need for these rules given.

This example deals with "Unsafe Play" (e.g. pupils karate kicking in the play area. The rule is that: -
"We keep our hands and feet to ourselves."

○ Asking, by name, the pupil or pupils who are behaving in this way to come over to you (away from their "audience").

○ After speaking to them, turn to chat to other pupils nearby. (By dropping eye contact and turning away, you give the pupils "face saving" time).

○ You might need to ask the pupils again, to compensate for "social deafness".

○ When the pupil/s walk over ask "What are you doing, fellas/lads?"

○ Then say what you saw, (e.g. "I saw you karate kicking, high kicks, for several minutes, fighting etc.)

○ Then remind them of the rule for "Safe Play".

○ As the pupils return to play, maybe say something positive, but which reminds them of the "Safe Play" rule (e.g. skilful kicking, but save it for the Karate Club).

14

"LETTER TO PARENTS" SYSTEM

This can be a very useful system, particularly for stopping the use of unacceptable and abusive language.

For older pupils

○ Make pupils write down exactly what they said and the circumstances which caused them to say it on a sheet with headings: - (See photocopiable example page 16)
○ Name............
○ Date..............
○ Describe in detail what you said ....
○ The circumstances which caused you to use inappropriate language........................
○ Pupil's signature....................................
○ Teacher's comments............................
○ Teacher's signature............................

○ Seal it in an envelope, write the parent's name and address on it.

○ Pin it up where the pupil can see it.

○ Tell the pupils that if there is another incident, the letter will be posted to the parent.

For younger pupils

○ An adult can scribe for them.
○ They can sign that it is a true report of what happened.

Dear Parent,

There was an incident at school today which involved your child using unacceptable language. Your child has been asked to complete this letter as a record of his/her behaviour.

Name...

Date of incident..

Describe in detail what you said, (including unacceptable or "swear" words).

....

....

....

....

What caused you to use inappropriate and unacceptable language?

....

....

....

....

Pupil's signature..

Teacher's comments...

....

....

....

Teacher's signature...

"STOP THE FIGHTING" REPORTS

This can be a very useful system, particularly as the written report makes it less likely that the story will have changed by the time the pupil gets home.

For older pupils

○ After the fight has been stopped, give each pupil a sheet to fill in.
Headings should include:- (See photocopiable example page 18)

  • Describe the problem
  • Why did you choose this behaviour?
  • How did your behaviour affect others?
  • What will happen if you continue to act in this way?
  • What can we do to reach a solution we can all live with?

○ Each pupil should read what he has written out loud so the other pupil/s can hear.

○ The teacher should then initiate discussion, focussing on the solution, not the conflict.

For younger pupils

○ An adult can scribe for them
○ They can sign that it is a true report of what happened.

"STOP THE FIGHTING" REPORT

Name

Date

Describe the problem/what happened

Why did you choose this behaviour?

How did your behaviour affect other people?

What will happen if you continue to behave in this way?

What can we do to reach a solution we can all live with?

Pupil's Signature

FIVE CARD STOP

This can be a very useful system, particularly as it hands responsibility for changing the behaviour over to the pupil.

It can be used for helping pupils who are persistently: -
- Making inappropriate noises
- Swearing

O   On 5 cards (the size of playing cards) write a number on each, from 1 to 5.

O   Explain to the pupils that these cards will be given to anyone who disrupts others by making inappropriate noises or if you hear them swearing.

O   Make sure that the pupil involved in misbehaving understands that when all the cards have been used, there will be a consequence.

O   Make sure the pupil knows the consequence and that this is something meaningful.

O   When a pupil makes an inappropriate noise, or you hear him swearing, give him all 5 cards.

O   Immediately remove the first card and tell him that he has lost this one for the inappropriate noise / abusive words you have just heard.

O   Make sure that if the pupil loses all his cards, the consequence is carried out.

"GIVE ME FIVE" ATTENTION GRABBER

This can be very useful for getting children's attention when you want to give instructions, start the lesson or tell them something important. It can be used during carpet time or when the children are working at their tables.

○ Like all systems, time and effort needs to be put into teaching the children how to use it.

○ Teach pupils to respond when you say **"Give me five!"**

1. All eyes are watching.

2. All ears are listening.

3. All mouths are silent.

4. All hands are still.

5. All feet are still.

GIVE ME FIVE!

○ A poster displayed prominently will remind children what the five points mean.

○ Adults can quickly point to the various parts of the body.

○ Children can hold up one hand, fingers outstretched to show that they are ready, before putting hand still in laps.

"RED, AMBER, GREEN" "DOT" SYSTEM

This can be a very useful for quietening noisy classes, as its use does not add to the noise levels.

○   To develop the red, amber, green "dot" system effectively, time and effort needs to be put into training and practice.

○   Tell pupils:-

   • That 3 levels of sound are allowed in your classroom and these are indicated by the colour of dots which are displayed where all can see them.

   • **Red** - no talking at all, silence.

   • **Amber** – enough talking to get a task completed (low to medium noise level).

   • **Green** – pupils may talk freely and have a normal conversation level (not shouting!)

HOW TO USE THIS BOOK

In this section you will find a description of the problem behaviour.

In this box you will find a list of possible reasons the problem behaviour may occur. It is by no means an exhaustive list and there may be many other reasons a child may be behaving inappropriately.

Things to try . . . .

In these boxes are approaches to try to tackle the problem behaviour.

If you are unsure of what the approach is, discuss with a colleague before using it or try a different method first.

Not all approaches will work with every child. Try approaches which have not been tried before.

Some of the approaches may seem a bit radical or unusual. Try to be open minded and positive with whichever approach you try.

In this section you will find a little note, which will encourage you to think about the behaviour you are targeting, or a motivational message.

Be confident with whichever method you use. Be patient and consistent.

SECTION TWO

Inside

CONTENTS – SECTION TWO

ANNOYING PEERS

SOME PUPILS PERSIST IN ANNOYING PEERS, DISTRACTING THEM FROM GETTING ON WITH THEIR WORK

WHY?

- They may not know that they are doing it.
- The work may be too difficult.
- They may not find the work interesting.
- They may have unresolved issues with their peers.
- They may be trying to make social contact and be unaware that it is not an appropriate time to do this.

Things to try . . .

Make sure the child knows what is expected of him.

Seat child near an adult who can encourage the child to stay on task.

Praise pupils who get on with their work.

Sit the child where he cannot easily have contact with peers.

Praise the child when he works independently.

REMEMBER! We all lack concentration at times.

Agree a private code word with the pupil. When the child behaves inappropriately use it to remind him, without drawing attention to the behaviour.

ANSWERING BACK

SOME PUPILS MAKE 'SMART' COMMENTS OR CHALLENGE THE ADULT

WHY?

- They may not know that this behaviour is unacceptable.
- They may be used to challenging adults.
- They may have gained attention from peers in the past in this way and want to continue.
- It has become a habit.
- They may feel they have a genuine grievance.

Things to try . . .

Restate the rules for acceptable behaviour.

Call the pupil aside for a quieter one-to-one word, without an audience.

Give a clear choice, to remain in the class and work by the fair rules or face "Time Out".

REMEMBER! We can all feel we want to rebel against authority at times!

Put up a "Blocking hand" and tell the pupil you will speak to him later, when the lesson has ended, in his own time. Always follow up this behaviour.

BREAKING PENCIL

SOME PUPILS PERSISTENTLY BREAK THEIR PENCILS SO THEY CAN SHARPEN THEM

WHY?

- They may be unable to do the work set, so want to waste time.
- Their hands may be tired and they want a break from writing. (Some say that it is inappropriate for young pupils to grip a pencil for too long).
- They may want the adult attention this behaviour will gain.
- This behaviour may previously have gained attention from peers and they wish this to continue.

Things to try . . .

Seat the child near an adult who can remind him to be careful.

Ensure that the adult sharpens the pencil for the pupil.

Make sure that the pencil is not one which breaks easily.

Give pupils pens to write with.

Ensure the work is at the correct level, so the child is well motivated.

REMEMBER! We are all reluctant to work at times!

Give the pupil several pencils, so that when one breaks he can still continue his work.

29

CALLING OUT

WHY?

- They may not be clear about what is expected of them.
- They may have experience of not being listened to in the past.
- They may be worried that if they do not call out straight away, they will forget what they wanted to say.

Things to try . . .

Make sure the child knows what is expected of him.

Make a "cut out" of a hand, (maybe with the words "I need help please" on it). Laminate it, put onto a stick and keep on desk to hold up when help is needed.

Ask pupil at regular intervals if s/he needs help.

Praise pupils who put hands up.

Seat child near an adult (who can whisper to that pupil).

Reminder on classroom wall (get pupils to help to make the poster).

Ignore when they call out.

REMEMBER!
We can all be impatient at times!

Praise the child when s/he waits or puts up hand, immediately.

COPYING

WHY?

- They may think it is okay to copy or cheat in order to succeed.
- They may feel undervalued and lack confidence to attempt the work themselves.
- They may not have listened to the instructions.
- Looking at others' work has become a habit.
- They may be 'checking' their own work.

Things to try . . .

Explain to the child that the behaviour is unacceptable and give reasons.

Have a class discussion of fair and unfair and why it is unfair to copy or use other people's ideas.

Provide opportunities for group work where pupils can express and share their views and ideas.

Have an independent working area. Sit children there when they are most likely to copy. Make it a pleasant, peaceful area that is productive to learning.

DAMAGING EQUIPMENT

SOME CHILDREN WILL DELIBERATELY BREAK CLASS EQUIPMENT

WHY?
- They may not have been taught to respect other people's property.
- They may be jealous.
- They may be clumsy.
- They may be angry.
- They may be seeking attention.

Things to try . . .

Give children an opportunity to borrow small class items.

Have an area where all equipment is safely kept and a monitor responsible for this area.

Have a lesson on the responsibility of looking after class equipment.

If you see a child getting angry, discreetly remove breakable objects from around him.

Allow children to take class items home on a rota basis.

Praise and reward children who are careful with equipment.

REMEMBER! It is difficult for children to vent their anger in appropriate ways.

Check the equipment used by pupils who are prone to this behaviour. Do this at the start and end of each lesson.

DAY DREAMING

WHY?

- They may be worried about something.
- They may not find the work interesting and so "switch off".
- They may be tired.
- They may be too hot and so lose concentration.

Things to try . . .

Make sure you have his full attention before giving instructions.

If you think the child is "day dreaming" say his name, then ask a question or tell him something, to gain his attention.

Make sure the child knows what is expected of him.

Seat the child near an adult who can help him stay on task.

Praise pupils who listen well.

Praise pupils who get on with their work.

Say the pupil's name, prior to asking a question or telling him something.

REMEMBER! We all have "off days" when we find it hard to concentrate on the task in hand!

Try to make the work interesting so he is motivated.

Make sure the room is not too hot.

33

DISRUPTING GROUP WORK

IT IS DIFFICULT FOR SOME PUPILS TO WORK IN A GROUP WITHOUT CAUSING DISRUPTION

WHY?

- They may have limited previous experience of group situations and not have developed such skills as turn-taking and sharing attention.
- They may feel threatened by other members of the group and may not have the confidence to participate in group work.
- They may find it difficult to differentiate between work time and social time.
- They may get excited and easily led by the presence of peers.
- They may enjoy being the centre of attention and want to uphold a reputation.

Things to try . . .

Introduce the idea of group work with a discussion of 'unwritten rules' which operate within a group.

Teach turn-taking skills in a class situation.

Start with small groups, possibly even pairs and build up gradually to larger groups.

Seat potentially disruptive children next to a teacher or other adult within the group.

Try grouping children of different abilities and different peer groups.

Allocate group leaders. Potentially disruptive children should be given chance to take on this role.

Give groups an 'identity' with each member having a part. E.g., CAR group, 1 pupil is the engine, another the wheels etc.

Gradually build up the time disruptive children spend in the group. Start by allowing them to join in the last five minutes. Only when this is successful should the time be increased.

REMEMBER! Value each child's opinion.

FIDGETING

SOME PUPILS CONSTANTLY FIDGET AND DISRUPT OTHERS

WHY?
- They may not know that they are doing it.
- They may be kinaesthetic learners and need to touch things.
- They may not be interested in the work.
- They may be one of those pupils who find sitting still difficult.
- They may be agitated about something which is worrying them.

Things to try . . .

Make sure the pupil is comfortable.

Praise the child when he sits appropriately.

Praise pupils who sit still and listen.

Make sure the child knows what is expected of him.

Give him something to "fidget with" (e.g. a small piece of modelling material).

Make sure that activities are varied so the pupil gets some chance to be active.

Seat child near an adult (who can whisper to that pupil).

REMEMBER! We can all be restless at times!

Try to make sure the task is interesting and the pupil is well motivated.

36

FREQUENTLY ASKING TO GO TO THE TOILET

WHY?

- They may be afraid to ask, or leave it too late.
- They may be too busy playing and forget.
- They may ask often because they do not want to do the work set.
- They may have a real reason for wanting to go very often.

Things to try . . .

Check that there is no medical problem.

Make sure children know that it is okay to go whenever they need to, as long as you always know where they are.

Use the "Teddy" idea.
- ❏ Have 1, 2, or 3 (depending on the size of your class) teddies, placed in a corner of the room.
- ❏ When the child needs to go to the toilet, he takes the teddy and sits it in his chair, replacing it in the corner, on his return.
- ❏ In this way you can regulate the number of pupils who have gone to the toilet at any one time.

*this will only be effective if you know where the children are sitting, not for "free play".

REMEMBER!
We all have "off days" when we find it hard to concentrate on the task in hand!

Discreetly remind children who may have "accidents" to go to the toilet when necessary.

37

GETTING THE CLASS QUIET

PUPILS SOMETIMES COLLECTIVELY MAKE A LOT OF NOISE WHEN YOU WANT TO SPEAK, OR START THE LESSON

WHY?

- They have something they want to say to their friends.
- Because others are talking, they have to talk louder.
- They may not have seen that you want their attention.

Things to try...

Do not add to the noise level, it will only make you more anxious.

Train the pupils to stop talking and copy you when you put your hand in the air.

Ask pupils to put their fingers on their noses, their shoulders, their heads etc.

Tell students to hold their breath while you count to 5. (You can do this several times at the start of a lesson, telling pupils that it will make them calm, yet their minds alert).

Develop the red, amber, green "dot" system. (See page 21).

REMEMBER! Most people like a good chat with their friends!

Teach pupils to respond when you say "Give me five!" (See page 20).

LINING UP AT THE CLASSROOM DOOR

PUPILS SOMETIMES BEHAVE INAPPROPRIATELY WHEN THEY ARE LINING UP WAITING TO GO INTO CLASS

WHY?

- Large numbers of pupils, when unsupervised, tend to be unruly.
- They may not know what is expected of them.
- They are still carrying on the play from outside school.
- They may have unresolved issues from the outside play time.
- They have to wait too long.
- They may not like peers being so close to them in the line, so push them etc.
- Because others are talking, they have to talk louder.

Things to try . . .

Provide adequate supervision.

Make sure they do not have to wait for long.

Encourage them to line up leaving a space between each pupil.

Ensure that pupils know the appropriate behaviour/noise levels for when they are inside.

If noise levels are unacceptable, play a few games, e.g.
- ❏ Simon says . . .
- ❏ I spy
- ❏ Everybody do this . . .
- ❏ Put your finger on your . . . .

REMEMBER!
We can all be impatient when there is nothing to do.

HURTING OTHERS

SOME CHILDREN WILL FIND OPPORTUNITIES TO HURT OTHER CHILDREN IN THE CLASSROOM

WHY?

- They could be seeking revenge on someone for an earlier incident.
- They may be frustrated by another child's actions.
- They may not have the appropriate skills to get something they want or need from another child.
- They may wish to be punished, e.g. sent out, in order to avoid work.
- They may be trying to attract adult attention but not have the skills to do it appropriately.

Things to try . . .

Have a zero tolerance policy of aggressive behaviour of any kind, including language, gestures and actions. Be consistent with the consequences.

If behaviour is persistent speak to the child before the lesson. Explain that you have noticed their behaviour and it will not be accepted.

Provide plenty of opportunities for children to resolve problems that may have occurred at playtime or earlier in the lesson.

If aggression is shown towards a particular pupil, pair the children up for fun activities. It is important that when this is done pupils are closely supervised.

Encourage the child to think about what positive uses hands and feet have. Children could draw round their hands and feet and fill with their ideas. Draw attention to these occasionally or when you think an incident may occur.

Minimise movement around the classroom. Most children are opportunists, so removing opportunity often removes temptation.

REMEMBER!
Expect pupils to behave well and often they will!

41

MAKING INAPPROPRIATE NOISES

SOME PUPILS MAKE INAPPROPRIATE NOISES WHEN OTHERS ARE TRYING TO LISTEN OR GET ON WITH THEIR WORK

WHY?
- They may not know that they are doing it.
- They may not know that they are disrupting others.
- They may have gained attention from peers in the past in this way and want to continue.
- It has become a habit.

Things to try . . .

Praise pupils who are getting on quietly with their work.

Make sure the child knows what is expected of him.

Seat the child near an adult (who can whisper to that pupil).

Seat pupil where he cannot see peers who may be encouraging the behaviour.

Ignore the noises, but talk to the pupil about his work, distracting him.

REMEMBER! We all have "bad days" when we are frustrated and may feel like being noisy!

Try the "5 card stop" idea. See page 19.

42

SOME PUPILS SEEM TO LACK MOTIVATION TO BEGIN WORK

WHY?

- They may not value school work in the same way as other pupils.
- They may not consider the work important or interesting.
- They may consider the work is too difficult and be afraid of failure.
- They may be influenced by peer pressure, where completing work is not seen as a positive thing.
- They may be used to getting work wrong so have no desire to repeat this experience.

Things to try . . .

Make sure the work is not too difficult.

Make sure the work is not too easy so that the pupil thinks it is not worth doing.

Make sure he knows how much he needs to do.

Break the work down into small steps. He can show you each time he completes one.

Give pupil an "egg" timer. He must work when the sand is running out and when it has stopped, you will look at how much he has completed.

Help pupils set and achieve goals for the work and praise when each is completed.

Seat child near an adult (who can help).

Praise pupils who begin work promptly.

Use a reward system, (e.g. a marble dropped into a jar) when the pupil begins work promptly.

REMEMBER! Starting a task is always the hardest part!

NOT PAYING ATTENTION

IT IS DIFFICULT FOR SOME CHILDREN TO PAY ATTENTION TO THE TEACHER

WHY?

- There may be an underlying problem causing short attention span e.g. poor diet, hearing or sight problems, poor sleep patterns etc.
- They may be distracted by noises, sights or smells.
- They may be worrying about problems outside the classroom.
- They may not be interested in the subject matter.
- They may find it uncomfortable to sit for long periods of time.
- They may be listening but not have the skills to demonstrate this.
- They may not have the skills needed to maintain attention or have many opportunities to practise these skills.

Things to try . . .

Devise a class 'signal' to gain attention, such as finger on nose, hand on shoulder etc.

Place great importance on good listening skills at every opportunity and demonstrate these yourself.

45

Keep listening activities short and interesting. During longer sessions have frequent breaks or change the style of your approach.

Accept that some children learn very little from listening and may need a 'doing' activity to complete whilst the lesson is going on.

Make paying attention a game for the child. E.g. make a mark on this paper every time I say 'going' or count how many times I point at the board.

Involve the child in the activity by giving them a role, e.g. page turner, character in a story, number in a sum etc.

REMEMBER!
Show enthusiasm and so will your pupils.

SOME CHILDREN FIND IT DIFFICULT TO SHARE EITHER THEIR OWN OR COMMUNAL BELONGINGS

WHY?

- They may have access to very few nice things.
- They may previously have been made to give up cherished possessions.
- Other people may not share with them.
- They may be scared of things being damaged or not returned.
- They may need to use the item again soon.

Things to try . . .

Demonstrate sharing whenever possible.

New or exciting items should be passed round each member of the class. Explain that they belong to everyone.

Discourage children from bringing their own possessions in from home.

Make sure each table or group has the same equipment.

Ensure that children know that they must return objects to a central area each time they finish using them.

Mark appropriate items with the class or group name.

Play "turn-taking" and sharing games.

REMEMBER!
Sharing with people who aren't your friends is difficult for us all

Praise and reward those children who share their belongings.

NOT SITTING STILL DURING CARPET TIME

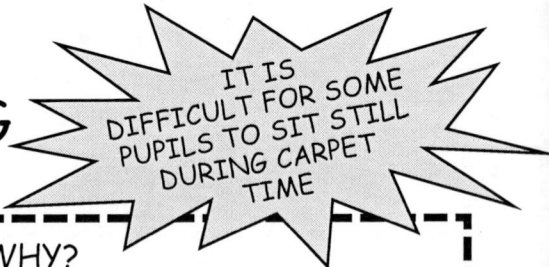

IT IS DIFFICULT FOR SOME PUPILS TO SIT STILL DURING CARPET TIME

WHY?

- They may not have been taught the skill.
- They may find the surface uncomfortable.
- They may feel uncomfortable with peers sitting so close.
- They may not find the topic interesting.
- They may have a short attention span.
- They may be unaware their behaviour is inappropriate.

Things to try . . .

Make carpet time interesting and fun, keeping children involved.

Make a bright star from yellow paper, laminate it and give to pupil. *"Today . . . you are going to be a star and sit on this star".*

Encourage children to "spread out" using all available space.

Seat child next to you on a chair.
"You be special and sit close to me."
"You be my assistant and turn the pages of the book".

Catch the child sitting well and praise immediately and often, for sitting still.

Seat all children on chairs.

Give the child something to occupy his hands while he is listening, (a small piece of plasticine is ideal). Explain to the child the reason for this.

Ignore the behaviour but praise those near the child, who are sitting still.

REMEMBER!
Persist - it takes time to change a learned behaviour.

NOT TELLING THE TRUTH

SOME CHILDREN FIND IT DIFFICULT TO TELL THE TRUTH

WHY?
- They may be unaware of the consequences.
- They may not want to admit to having done something wrong.
- It may be a habit.
- They may exaggerate or lie to be popular with peers.
- They may think it is what you want to hear.
- They may have an overactive imagination.

Things to try . . .

Ignore "white lies" or exaggerations and show interest in facts.

Encourage the child to write reason or excuses in a "Truth Book".

Encourage the child to truthfully retell situations you have witnessed.

Provide the child with a 'Story Book', where he can use his imagination productively.

Speak to the child individually about his responsibility to tell the truth.

REMEMBER!
We all sometimes say what we want others to hear.

Hold up a truth signifier when you think a child is lying or exaggerating.

50

PROBLEMS IN CORRIDORS AND TOILET AREAS

SOME PUPILS ALWAYS SEEM TO GET INTO TROUBLE IN THE CORRIDORS OR IN THE TOILET AREAS

WHY?

- There may be inadequate supervision.
- There may be no guidelines or rules.
- Pupils may not feel safe.
- Pupils may not know what is expected of them in these areas.

Things to try . . .

Have an agreed school policy to ensure consistency of discipline throughout all the areas.

Negotiate positive rules.

Make sure at the start of each term that pupils know the agreed guidelines.

Discuss the idea of consequences when agreed rules are broken.

Ask pupils periodically:-
- ❏ *Whether they are having trouble with people or other things in these areas.*
- ❏ *Answers should be written, or the questions asked individually.*
- ❏ *Confidentiality is vital.*

REMEMBER! It is impossible to follow rules that don't exist.

Having "Corridor Supervisors" (appointed on a rotating basis) who can make sure that rules are adhered to etc.

REFUSING TO WORK INDEPENDENTLY

SOME PUPILS APPEAR UNABLE TO WORK ON THEIR OWN

WHY?
- They may be unsure of how to complete the task.
- The work may be too difficult or too easy.
- They may not find the topic interesting.
- They may be afraid of failure and need reassurance that they can succeed.
- They may have built up a reputation with their peers for "not being a good worker" and be afraid to change.

Things to try . . .

Break the task down into small units - pupil to put up hand when the section has been completed.

Sit near adult.

Make sure pupils know what is expected and how to complete the work.

Break time down into small units so pupils work, for example, for 5 minutes at a time without looking up.

Sit pupil on own table facing away from peers who may distract him.

Pupils can be given two clock faces and can draw on one the start time and on the other, the time they will finish.

REMEMBER! We all have days when we are less inclined to do our best!

Offer reassurance throughout the task.

RUBBING OUT

SOME PUPILS WILL PERSIST IN RUBBING OUT, SOMETIMES UNTIL THEY MAKE HOLES IN THE PAPER

WHY?

- They may not like what they have done and want to eradicate it.
- They may be afraid of failure.
- They may think the work is wrong and fear being "told off".
- They may not find the work interesting, are bored and want something else to do.

Things to try . . .

If rubbers are to be used make sure they are of a good quality and are kept clean.

Use rubbers only for "final drafts" or where work is for display purposes.

Make sure that pupils know that rubbing out until they make a hole in the paper is unacceptable.

Convince pupils that errors are a good thing, that they help you to make changes.

Train pupils to put a single line through errors instead of rubbing out.

Ban all rubbers.

REMEMBER!
No-one likes others to see their mistakes!

Make sure that the pupil can do the work, so he does not need to worry about making too many errors.

RUNNING IN CORRIDOR

SOME PUPILS SEEM TO FIND IT DIFFICULT TO WALK UP THE CORRIDOR AND PERSIST IN RUNNING

WHY?

- They may not know that running is unacceptable.
- They may not realise the safety implications.
- They may need to be more active.
- They may really be in a hurry.
- A long stretch of corridor is very tempting, especially if you think no-one is watching you.

Things to try . . .

Make sure the child knows what is expected of him.

Have clear discussions about safety and possible accidents.

Depending on what the corridor is used for, place "obstacles" (e.g. table with plant or a display of books).

Send the child back, watch him walk and give praise for walking.

Always praise pupils who are walking sensibly.

Place reminders along the corridor, (pupils can assist with making the posters).

Make a "Footprint trail" for pupils to walk along.

REMEMBER!
Although there are safety implications, this "problem" should be kept in perspective and not made into more of an issue than it needs.

Catch walking, a pupil who is often in trouble for running and praise immediately.

RUSHING WORK

SOME CHILDREN WILL RUSH THEIR WORK TO FINISH BEFORE OTHERS

WHY?
- They may think that working fast means working hard.
- They may think it makes them look clever.
- They may not find the work challenging enough.
- They may have a short attention span.
- They may want to do another activity.
- They may have a poor concept of time.

Things to try . . .

Explain to the child how much time he has to complete the work and show him this on a clock.

Provide enough work to fill the time, even if the child works quickly.

Praise children who are working slowly and carefully and whose work is well presented.

Divide work up into smaller sections and hand out at set times.

REMEMBER! Children are highly affected by what their peers think of them.

Put markers on the child's work with the time he should reach that point.

SHOUTING OUT

SOME PUPILS PERSISTENTLY SHOUT OUT ANSWERS TO THE TEACHER'S QUESTIONS

WHY?
- They may forget that they have to raise their hands.
- They may be worried that if they do not answer immediately they will forget.
- They may be trying to impress their peers by being 'clever.'

Things to try . . .

Use whiteboards for children to write the answer on and to hold up quietly when they know it.

Use children's names before and after asking questions.

Thank the child for his answer then move on to another child to answer.

Expect all children to be ready with the answer. Explain to the children that they should no longer put their hand up to answer questions.

Ignore the child's responses and ask other children who have their hands up. Praise this behaviour.

Ask the child to answer the first question and explain that he has answered once and to give other children a chance.

REMEMBER!
We are all eager to answer questions we know the answers to.

When the child displays desired behaviour, praise IMMEDIATELY and invite the child to answer the question.

SWEARING

SOME PUPILS WILL USE ABUSIVE, UNACCEPTABLE LANGUAGE IN SCHOOL

WHY?

- They use this language outside school.
- They may not have been taught that it is unacceptable.
- It has become a habit, part of their usual vocabulary.
- They may not have any other way to express their frustration.

Things to try . . .

Don't over react. Turn the incident into a learning experience, discussing who is hurt by it, who is insulted by it etc.

Make sure the child knows that swearing and hurting people with words, is not acceptable.

Teach more acceptable methods of expressing feelings.

Use the "Five card" control technique. (See page 19)

For older pupils use the "Letter to Parents" System. (See page 15)

REMEMBER!
Persist – habits can be hard to break.

SWINGING ON CHAIR

SOME PUPILS WILL CONSTANTLY SWING ON THEIR CHAIRS, MAKING IT DIFFICULT FOR OTHERS TO PASS SAFELY

WHY?

- They may not know they are doing it.
- They may not know that it can be dangerous, both to themselves, if they slip off and to others who may catch themselves on the chair leg as they pass by.
- They may have gained attention from peers in the past in this way and want to continue.
- It has become a habit.
- He may find the chair uncomforatble after an extended period of time.

Things to try . . .

Make sure the child knows what is expected of him.

Seat child near an adult (who can whisper to that pupil).

Tell and then remind him of the dangers both to himself and to others.

Praise pupils who sit appropriately.

Seat him where he cannot get peer attention for repeating the behaviour.

REMEMBER! We can all be restless at times!

Vary activities so that pupils are not sitting for too long.

58

UNMOTIVATED OR APATHETIC

SOME PUPILS APPEAR TO LACK MOTIVATION AND ARE APATHETIC ABOUT ALL SCHOOL WORK

WHY?

- They may come from a background where school / academic achievement is not valued.
- They may not consider school work important or interesting.
- They may consider the work is too dificult and be afraid of failure.
- They may be influenced by peer pressure, where enjoying work is not seen as a positive thing.
- They may be used to getting work wrong so have no desire to repeat this experience.

Things to try . . .

Talk to the pupil about how he feels about school and work.

Make sure the work is not so difficult that the pupil will fail.

Make sure the work is not so easy so that the pupil thinks it is not worth doing.

Break the work down into small steps. He can show you each time he completes one.

Help pupils set and achieve goals for the work and praise when each is completed.

Make sure he knows how much he needs to do.

Use a reward system, (e.g. a marble dropped into a jar) when the pupil gets on with his work.

Seat child near an adult he likes and who can prompt and praise.

REMEMBER!
Most of us need help with some tasks some times.

WANDERING ABOUT

SOME PUPILS FIND IT DIFFICULT TO STAY IN THEIR SEAT AND SO WILL WANDER AROUND THE CLASSROOM

WHY?

- They may be interested in the environment.
- They may not understand the work they have to do.
- They may be tired and wandering about to keep awake.
- They may find it uncomfortable to sit for long periods of time.
- They may not know how to gain attention in appropriate ways.
- There may be unresolved issues with peers.

Things to try . . .

Alternate the seating arrangements so the child has the opportunity to experience different parts of the classroom.

Allow the child to explore the classroom at appropriate and set times, perhaps whilst the rest of the class are not present.

Provide the child with interesting activities on his table that can be done when he gets stuck or frustrated or has finished the set task. Praise him for getting on with these.

Praise and reward the child after a set period of time for remaining in his seat.

Each time the child gets up from his seat, approach him and guide him back to his seat, without mentioning the behaviour and focus him back on task.

Provide the child with an egg timer or stop watch on his table. Set this for an achievable amount of time and explain that when the time is up he must come and show you his work. Extend the period of time gradually.

REMEMBER!
Have high expectations
of all pupils.

SECTION THREE

Outside

CONTENTS - SECTION THREE

AGGRESSIVE OR THREATENING BEHAVIOUR

SOME PUPILS USE THREATENING OR AGGRESSIVE BEHAVIOUR TOWARDS OTHER PUPILS

WHY?

- They may feel threatened themselves.
- They may want to uphold a reputation.
- They may have had little experience of positive play and social interactions.
- They may not have the social skills to approach people appropriately and make friends.
- They may be "sticking up" for someone.

Things to try . . .

Demonstrate appropriate social skills and body language. Explain to the child how this is different from his.

Formally introduce pupils to different sets of friends and suggest appropriate play for them.

Try to humour the child out of his threatening stance. Be careful not to humiliate or ridicule.

At an appropriate time, spend time with the pupil in front of a mirror, encouraging him to adopt his normal playground attitude and how this can be changed into a more approachable way of presenting himself.

Discuss with the child individually how others perceive his behaviour.

Provide opportunities for children to discuss incidents or situations that may have angered them.

REMEMBER!
Our facial expressions don't always reflect our thoughts and feelings.

Be aware of ongoing disputes on the playground and monitor relevant children closely.

67

CLINGING TO STAFF

SOME PUPILS WILL NOT JOIN IN WITH THE PLAY OF OTHERS AND ARE RELUCTANT TO LEAVE STAFF

WHY?

- They may not be used to playing with other children.
- They may be uncertain of what is expected of them.
- They may be shy and lack confidence.
- Another pupil may be intimidating him and he is afraid to tell staff.

Things to try . . .

Talk discreetly to the child's parent/s to see if they know if there is a problem.

Talk to the pupil to find out what the problem is.

Find a "friend" who the pupil can relate to and either sit them together for activities or give them a shared "job" to do at playtime.

Make sure pupils know that they can come to you with any concerns.

Set up a "buddy" system for outside play, where an older pupil takes responsibility for a younger pupil.

REMEMBER! We all lack confidence at certain times and need a little reassurance!

68

CONSTANTLY TELLING TALES

SOME PUPILS ARE ALWAYS COMPLAINING ABOUT THE BEHAVIOUR OF OTHERS

WHY?

- They may need attention and not know how to gain it.
- They may have a genuine grievance and be afraid.
- They may not have anyone to play with and have been "pushed out" when trying to make social contact.

Things to try . . .

Make sure pupils know that they can come to you with any genuine concerns.

Talk to the pupil to find out what the problem is.

Give the responsibility to the pupils. Try, "Okay, so they took your ball. What can you say to them to get it back?" Stand nearby for support while they try to solve the problem themselves.

Draw all participants aside and remind about the rules for "Fair play".

REMEMBER! We all have "bad" days when everything others do seems wrong!

Give pupils who have difficulties during outside play times, a job to do.

69

FIGHTING

WHY?

- They may not know any other way to resolve the issue.
- They may feel that no-one cares whether they fight or not.
- They may see it as a way to "keep in" with peers.
- They may get reinforcement from their peers when they fight.
- They may see it as a "fearless" thing to do, when they are really afraid.

Things to try . . .

Make sure pupils know that fighting will not be tolerated. Give frequent reminders.

If you consider that an argument could lead to a fight, separate pupils, give them each a job to do or send them on a message to different areas.

Separate the pupils fighting or remove the cause of the trouble.

Watch for groups of pupils who may be "fuelling" an argument, encouraging pupils to fight.

Identify pupils who quickly become angry.

Train these pupils to manage their frustration by deep breathing, chanting quietly to themselves.

REMEMBER! We all get angry sometimes!

Use "Stop the fighting reports" (See page 17)

70

GENERAL PLAYGROUND PROBLEMS

THE PLAYGROUND SEEMS TO BE AN AREA WHERE MANY PUPILS EXPERIENCE PROBLEMS

WHY?

- The area may have no structure.
- There may be no guidelines or rules.
- Pupils may not feel safe.
- Pupils may not know how to use the area.

Things to try . . .

Create a structured physical environment, set up zones for specific activities, paint lines to identify zones.

Look at the sorts of activities pupils enjoy outside, for example:-Running games, playing with cars, skipping games, reading, clapping games etc. (see ideas in "Yards of Playground Fun" by Ann Preston.
ISBN 1 904 374 54 9).

Have a "Playground Committee" – members are responsible for playtimes.

Discuss the idea of consequences when agreed rules are broken.

Have "Playtime Supervisors", who can demonstrate how to play games, sort out disputes, etc.

REMEMBER! The outside area should be a fun place to enjoy physical activity!

Provide seating and shade.

LITTER

WHY?

- They may not see litter as a problem.
- Disposing of litter properly may not be a priority in their home environment.
- They may be used to someone else clearing up after them.
- They might not have been taught how to deal with litter.

Things to try...

Ask pupils to (safely) help you to pick up any litter.

Make sure that there are plenty of rubbish bins with small openings so that paper cannot fly out.

Ban all snacks except fruit.

Make sure pupils know that dropping litter will not be tolerated. Give frequent reminders.

Make sure that any snacks with wrappings have the pupil's name on so that the person dropping litter can be identified.

Pupils should eat all snacks inside school.

REMEMBER! Children will copy the behaviour of others!

If you actually see someone dropping litter, a non confrontational direction, such as "The bin's over there", is better than "Pick that up". If the pupil refuses, tell him you will deal with the problem later (not outside where he has a peer audience to spur him on).

72

NO ONE TO PLAY WITH

SOME PUPILS WILL NOT JOIN IN WITH THE PLAY OF OTHERS AND ARE RELUCTANT TO LEAVE STAFF

WHY?

- They may not be used to playing with other children.
- They may be uncertain of what is expected of them.
- They may be shy and lack confidence.
- Another pupil may be intimidating him and he is afraid to tell staff.

Things to try . . .

Talk to the pupil to find out what the problem is.

Make sure pupils know that they can come to you with any concerns.

Have a "Friendship Bench" where pupils who have no-one to play with can sit. When someone sees them there, they will invite them to join their game.

Find a "friend" who the pupil can relate to and either sit them together for activities or give them a shared "job" to do at playtime.

Have a "Friendship Club", where pupils can go to make friends prior to going outside to play.

REMEMBER!
We are all sometimes reluctant to return to work after a period of fun!

Set up a "Buddy" system for outside play, where an older pupil takes responsibility for a younger pupil.

73

PLAYING IN THE WRONG AREA

SOME PUPILS WILL PLAY IN AREAS THAT ARE OUT OF BOUNDS OR RESERVED FOR SPECIFIC TYPES OF PLAY

WHY?

- They may not know that they are not allowed there.
- They may want to be with friends who are allowed in other areas.
- They may be trying to draw attention to themselves.
- They may not understand why there are areas that are unsafe or allocated for specific play.
- They may be trying to spoil other people's games.

Things to try . . .

Encourage the child to draw a large map of the playground, marking on specific areas. This could be displayed in an appropriate place in school.

Mark the different areas of the playground with signs that children have made. These can be taken out and collected each playtime by monitors.

Approach the child and without mentioning that he is in the wrong place, prompt him back to an appropriate part of the playground.

Walk round every area of the playground with the child explaining which areas are for what use and the reasons for this. This could also be done with the whole class at the start of term.

Explicitly explain safety implications of playing in unsafe areas.

REMEMBER! It's exciting to go somewhere where we shouldn't be!

Spend time in each part of the playground every playtime.

Appoint playground monitors. Children who are prone to this behaviour should be given a chance to do this role.

74

REFUSING TO COME INTO SCHOOL

SOME PUPILS ARE RELUCTANT TO COME BACK INTO SCHOOL AT THE END OF PLAY TIME

WHY?

- They may not have realised that play time was coming to an end.
- They may be reluctant to stop their games.
- They may be reacting to peer pressure by behaving inappropriately.
- They may enjoy the adult/peer attention this behaviour gives.

Things to try . . .

Make sure pupils know that they can come to you with any unresolved issues.

Have an agreed signal to mark the end of the outside activities.

Make sure that all pupils are involved in activities.

Make sure all pupils know the procedure.

Teachers and assistants should meet pupils outside and play a ring game prior to going back to class.

Find out what the problem is.

If you know that refusal is a possibility, give him a job to do at the end of play, e.g.
- ❏ *Collect up equipment.*
- ❏ *Have responsibility for checking that everyone goes in.*
- ❏ *Help younger pupils walk into class.*

REMEMBER!
We are all sometimes reluctant to return to work after a period of fun!

RELUCTANT TO GO OUT TO PLAY

SOME PUPILS ARE RELUCTANT TO GO OUTSIDE AT BREAK TIMES

WHY?

- They may not have anyone to play with when they are outside.
- They may have had a bad experience.
- There may not be any activities on offer that they want to join in with.

Things to try . . .

Talk to the pupil to find out what the problem is.

Make sure that there are a variety of activities on offer. Not all pupils enjoy boisterous games. Activities might include:-

- ❏ *Dancing*
- ❏ *Playing with cars*
- ❏ *Colouring*
- ❏ *Reading*
- ❏ *Wordsearches*
- ❏ *Chasing bubbles*
- ❏ *Gardening*

Make sure pupils know that they can come to you with any concerns.

Give reluctant pupils a job, e.g.

- ❏ *Collecting up equipment.*
- ❏ *Having responsibility for checking that everyone goes in.*
- ❏ *Helping younger pupils walk into class.*

REMEMBER!
We are all reluctant to go into situations we don't enjoy!

76

RETURNING TO CLASS AFTER PLAYTIME

INAPPROPRIATE BEHAVIOUR OFTEN SEEMS TO OCCUR WHEN PUPILS ARE RETURNING TO CLASS AFTER BEING OUTSIDE

WHY?

- There may not be adequate supervision.
- Pupils have been reluctant to stop their games.
- They may be reacting to peer pressure by behaving inappropriately.
- There may be no guidelines or rules.

Things to try . . .

Observe the behaviour to see what the problems are.

Discuss the idea of consequences when agreed rules are broken.

Make sure all pupils know the procedure.

Have an agreed signal to mark the end of the outside activities.

Negotiate positive rules.

Paint class "circles" on the ground.

Teachers and assistants should meet their classes outside.

Adults can play a ring game with pupils prior to going back to class.

REMEMBER!
We are all sometimes reluctant to return to work after a period of fun!

Pupils can play "Follow my Leader" games when going in.

SPOILS OTHERS' GAMES

WHY?

- They may want to join in but don't know how to do this appropriately.
- They may have been "pushed out" of the game before.
- They may not know the rules of the game.
- They may be seeking attention.
- They may be jealous that others are having a good time.

Things to try . . .

Make sure there is enough equipment available.

Remind pupils about the fair play rule. Give frequent reminders.

Provide alternative activities.

Ensure that pupils know some of the strategies which can be used to prevent this happening. E.g.

- ❏ *Talk it over with the person.*
- ❏ *Invite them to join in your game.*
- ❏ *Try to stop the behaviour – "I don't like it when you....."*
- ❏ *Warn them "If you keep doing that, I shall have to tell the teacher"*

REMEMBER! We can all feel jealous when others are having a good time and we feel excluded!

78

SWEARING

WHY?

- They use this language when playing at home.
- They may think that because they are outside, that it is okay.
- It has become a habit, part of their usual vocabulary.
- They may not have any other way to express their frustration.
- They may want to identify with their peers, be part of a group which uses these words.

Things to try . . .

Make sure the child knows that swearing and hurting people with words, is not acceptable, inside school or outside in the playground.

Don't over react. Turn the incident into a learning experience, discussing who is hurt by it, who is insulted by it etc.

Teach more acceptable methods of expressing feelings.

Use the "Five card" control technique. (See page 19)

REMEMBER!
Persist – habits can be hard to break.

For older pupils use the "Letter to Parents" system. (See page 15)

79

TEASING

SOME PUPILS UPSET THEIR PEERS BY TEASING THEM

WHY?
- They may not know that this behaviour is unacceptable.
- They may be used to being teased themselves, so think that it is okay to do it to others.
- They may not know how much this can upset and hurt others.
- They may get reinforcement from their peers when they upset others in this way.

Things to try . . .

Make sure pupils know that teasing will not be tolerated. Give frequent reminders.

Watch for pupils who may be encouraging a pupil or pupils teasing others.

Provide alternative activities.

Make all pupils aware of some of the strategies they can use if they are teased.
- ❑ *Ignore and walk away.*
- ❑ *Talk it over with the person.*
- ❑ *Invite them to join in your game.*
- ❑ *Try to stop the behaviour – "I don't like it when you....."*
- ❑ *Warn them "If you keep doing that, I shall have to tell the teacher".*

REMEMBER!
When people are unkind, it really hurts us!

80

UNSAFE PLAY

SOME PUPILS PERSIST IN PLAYING IN A WAY WHICH MAY LEAD TO INJURY (E.G. KARATE KICKING)

WHY?

- They may not realise that they are putting themselves or others in danger.
- They may feel that no-one cares whether they keep to the rules or not.
- They may see it as a way to "keep in" with peers.
- They may get reinforcement from their peers when they behave in this way.

Things to try . . .

Make sure pupils know that unsafe play will not be tolerated. Give frequent reminders.

Make sure that you have a rule which covers this sort of play.
❏ E.g. "We keep our hands and feet to ourselves".

Watch for groups of pupils who may be encouraging pupils to play in an inappropriate way.

Deal with the pupil/s by using the playground management technique. (See page 14)

REMEMBER!
Children will copy behaviour they see on T.V., computer games etc.!

Identify pupils who are likely to play in this way and involve them in a game.

SECTION FOUR

Ideas for Rewarding

CONTENTS - SECTION FOUR

INDIVIDUAL REWARD SYSTEMS

WHAT ARE THESE FOR?

• These suggested 'Reward Systems' should be used only with those children who have a specific and persistent behaviour problem.
• These reward systems are most effective when used sparingly in classrooms for problem behaviour that has not lessened with any other approach.
• They have been designed to be motivational and attractive to children, but are basic enough to be easy to use.

WHAT THEY SHOULD NOT BE USED FOR?

• This approach should not be used as a 'quick fix' for children misbehaving in the classroom.
• Repetitive use of them diminishes their effectiveness, as does using them with more than a couple of children at the same time.
• They are not designed to be used as a bribe for children and rewards achieved at the end of the approach should be carefully thought out and should not necessarily be tangible or materialistic.
• It is important that these systems are not used to just try and get children to 'be good'.

HOW TO USE THEM . . .

- These charts should be used as part of a planned approach to tackling problem behaviour.
- Be open and honest with the child about why you are using this approach and gain their cooperation. This will increase the success of the reward system.
- It is important that the behaviour you wish to tackle is specific. A target should be agreed with the child, ensuring that it is challenging, achievable and phrased positively. Some examples of targets are;

'I will go to my seat within 30 seconds of coming in the classroom.'
'I will WALK down the corridor instead of running.'
'I will put my hand up to answer a question.'
'I will start my work 10 seconds after I sit down.'

- Once a target has been decided upon, encourage the child to choose one of the reward charts. This can then be copied on to card or coloured paper.
- The child should then write his own target in the space provided.
- The chart should then be placed where the child has easy access to it when the desired behaviour occurs.
- Some children are not comfortable with their peers knowing they are using a reward chart, while others may use it to 'show off' to their friends. These issues should be dealt with sensitively and taken into account when deciding where to place the chart. Responsibility should be given to the child to complete the chart himself.

- Where possible the chart should be coloured in immediately after the desired behaviour has occurred. Once all parts are coloured a reward should be given, see below for suggestions.
- Whilst using a reward system with individual children, sensitivity should be shown towards other children whose behaviour is consistently acceptable.
- It may be beneficial to explain to the class why you are using this approach and that it will be better for everyone in the class if behaviour is improved.

REWARD IDEAS

- Ideally pupils should be working towards feeling better about their behaviour and so ultimately the goal is that good behaviour itself is the reward. However, it may take time to achieve this, particularly in younger pupils.
- Simple items such as stickers, certificates, a mention in Assembly or letter home to parents are often enough to motivate and reward children.
- If a tangible reward is given, this should be small and given discreet. It is important that the child doesn't become dependent on rewards to achieve better behaviour.

REMEMBER...

Never use reward systems to punish a child or ridicule them about their behaviour. Remain positive about the approach even if it doesn't appear to be working. Persist and you too will be rewarded!

_____'s Reward Chart

My Target is _____

Each time you do this colour in 1 part of the caterpillar.

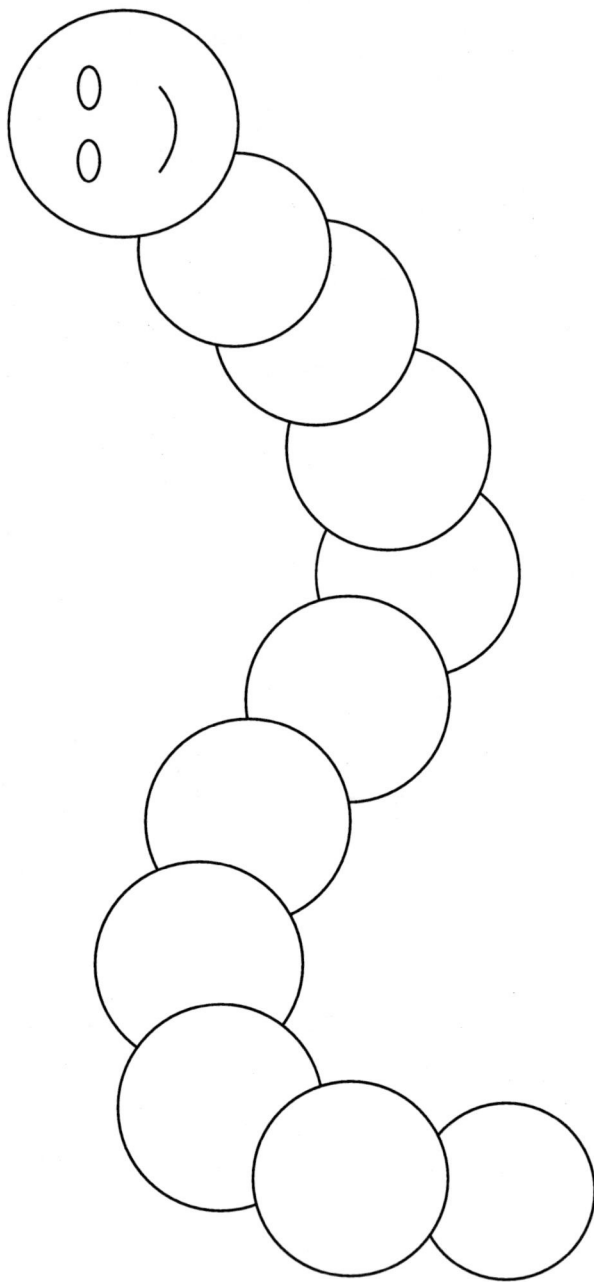

_____ 's Reward Chart

My Target is _____
Each time you do this colour in 1 of the happy faces.

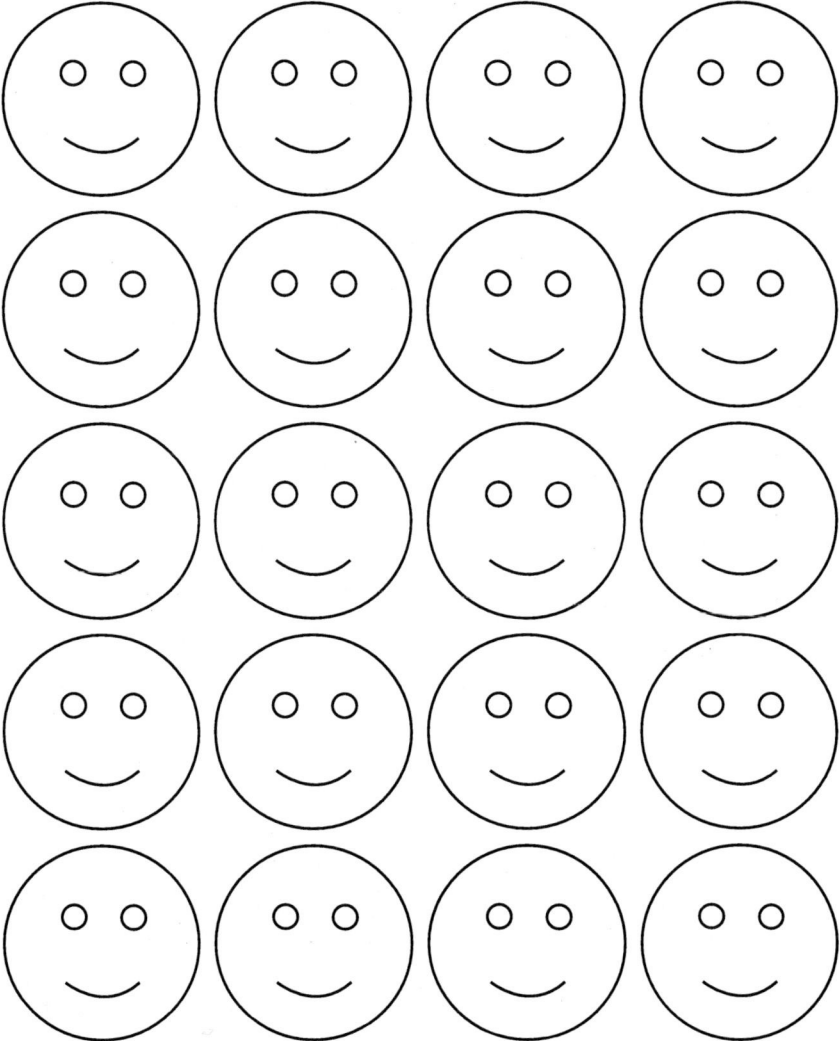

_____'s Reward Chart

My Target is _____

Each time you do this colour in 1 of the footballs to score a goal.

_____'s Reward Chart

My Target is _____

Each time you do this colour in 1 of the colours of the rainbow.

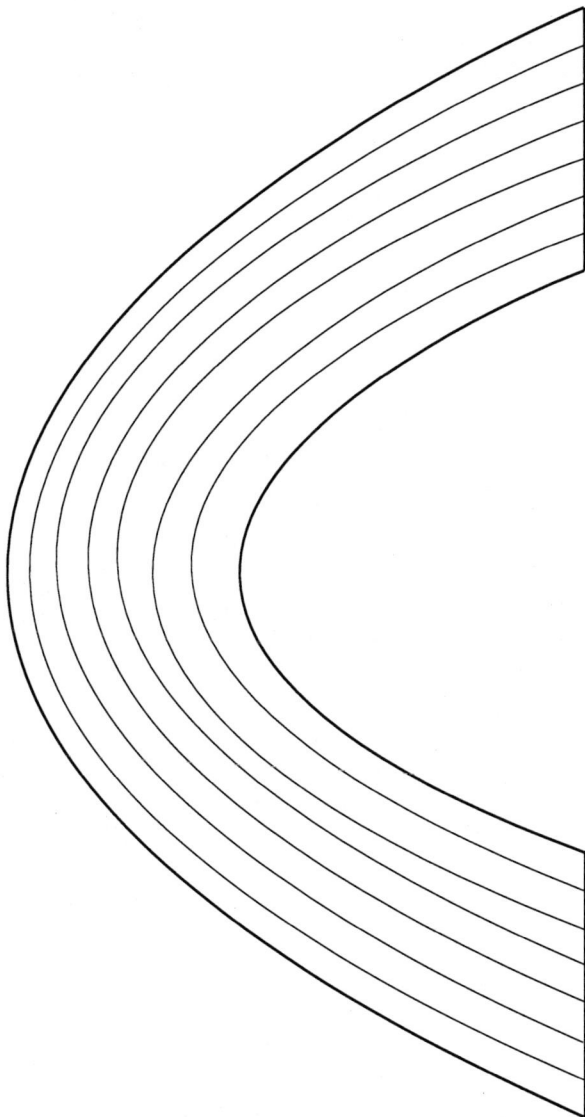

93

_____'s Reward Chart

My Target is _____

Each time you do this colour in 1 of the rays of sunshine.

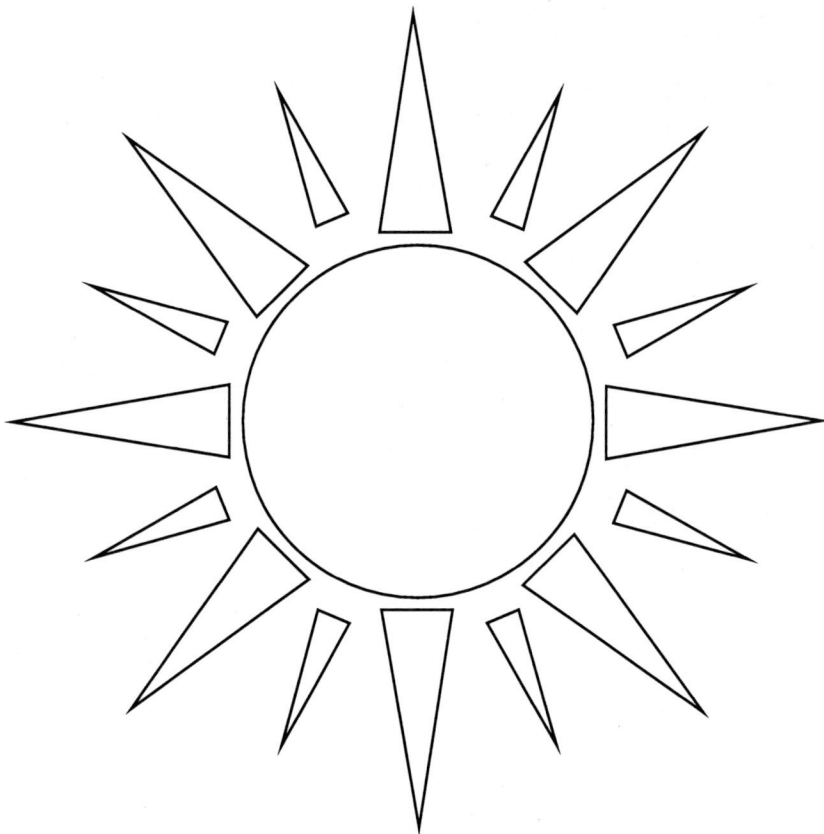

CLASS REWARD IDEAS

- Whether you use the "Pot of Gold" idea, the "Nuts and Bolts" or put marbles in a jar, you will need to have ideas for how to reward your class when they have achieved their goal and deserve "GOLDEN TIME".

Here are a few suggestions
- Extra playtime
- Watching a DVD/Video
- Ice creams
- A class cake
- Free choice of activities for one session
- Extra computer time
- A choice of art and craft activities
- Bringing a game from home to play with for a specified time.
- A lunchtime picnic (eating their usual lunch together in a special place, inside or outside)
- Non uniform day
- A cookery session

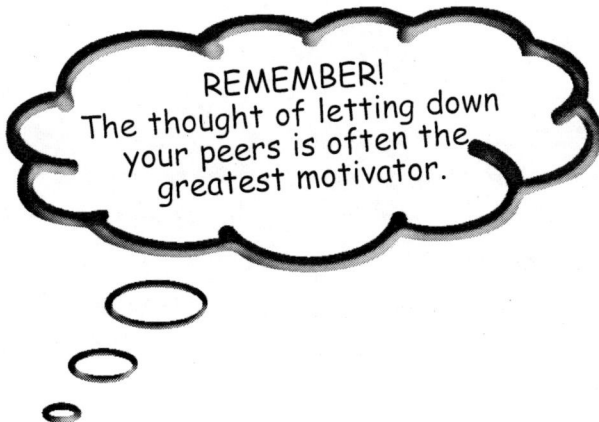

REMEMBER!
The thought of letting down your peers is often the greatest motivator.

THE POT OF GOLD

➤ You will need a container, which will hold about 50 medium sized stones or rocks.

➤ Spray the 50 or 60 rocks gold.

➤ Place the gold "nuggets" beside the pot.

➤ Pupils can place a golden nugget in the pot each time they do something you think needs rewarding.
This may be :-
❑ Doing a brilliant piece of work
❑ Getting 100% on a test
❑ Doing something helpful/kind for a class member
❑ Tidying something up without being asked
❑ Working co-operatively during PE

➤ Once the pot is full of gold, the pupils will receive a class reward.

These might include:
❑ Extra playtime
❑ Watching a DVD/Video
❑ Ice Creams
❑ Extra computer time
❑ A choice of art and craft activities
❑ Bringing a game from home to play with for a specified time
❑ A lunchtime picnic (eating their usual lunch together in a special place, inside or outside).

NUTS AND BOLTS

❋ This is a very old, but a tried and tested reward system.

❋ You will need a plastic/glass jar and enough nuts and bolts (of the same sizes) to fill the jar.

❋ Explain to the pupils that you will assess each day in terms of the quality of the learning which has taken place.

❋ If it has been a good day, you will add a bolt.

❋ If it has only been a moderately good day, you will add a nut (which takes up less space in the jar).

❋ If there is a day when the behaviour has not been good, so learning has not been as productive as it could have been, neither a nut or a bolt will be added.

❋ Once the jar is full, the pupils will receive a class reward.

These might include:
- ❏ Extra playtime
- ❏ Ice creams
- ❏ A cake for the class
- ❏ Extra computer time
- ❏ A choice of art and craft activities
- ❏ Bringing a game from home to play with for a specified time.

5 MINUTES FREE TIME NOTES

➤ This is a quick, efficient, low cost reward system, which will motivate pupils.

➤ The notes can be given for achievement, performing a specific task, or for helping peers.

➤ You must give pupils some guidelines as to when/how they can use the notes. (e.g. pupil may work for 5 minutes at the computer, read a book, do a wordsearch, draw a picture etc. while others are doing set tasks).

---

5 MINUTES FREE TIME

.... (The owner of this note)
     (Pupil's Name)

    has earned FIVE (5) minutes of free time

Awarded by ....
                (Teacher's Name)

Date ....

    *this note must be spent wisely in a supervised place

"LIKE" NOTES

✳ "Like" notes will lift the spirits of every member of the class.

✳ Each pupil is given pieces of paper (such as the one below) one for each member of the class.

✳ They write the names of the pupils and then what they like about that pupil.

✳ Pupils should be encouraged to think of qualities and deeds rather than physical attributes.

✳ When they are all completed, they are given out to the class members.

✳ Each pupil receives lots of "happy thoughts".

To ....

This is what I like about you:-

....

....

....
